Romance
Again

Dating after Divorce

David J Robertson

BY THE SAME AUTHOR

Marriage - Restoring our vision

Text copyright © David Robertson 2006
The author asserts the moral right to be
identified as the author of this work.

Published by
friendsfirst Publishing

PO Box 4853
Stratford-upon-Avon
CV37 1FZ

www.friends1st.co.uk

ISBN-13:   978-0-9552164-1-1
ISBN-10:   0-9552164-1-9

First published 2006
10 9 8 7 6 5 4 3 2 1 0

Designed and typeset by MATS Typesetting
Printed by J. H. Haynes & Co. Ltd., Sparkford
Cover design by David Lund Design.

Contents

Foreword 4

Preface 5

Introduction 7

Part 1: When we divorce 11

    Part 1 Introduction 13

1. Bereavement 15
2. Leaving the past 20
3. Dealing with the past 24

Part 2: When we develop new friendships 27

    Part 2 Introduction 29

4. Plenty more fish in the sea 31
5. Making contact 35
6. Falling in love again 41
7. Getting physical 46
8. Going public 49
9. Building on quicksand 52
10. Contemplating remarriage 56

Part 3: How a new relationship affects family life 61

    Part 3 Introduction 63

11. A child's perspective 65
12. Mentioning money 71

Conclusion: Cold feet or warm heart? 74

Resources 77

Foreword

This is a wise, readable, accessible and practical book – a book born out of the pain of personal experience of divorce, as well as the joy of risking dating and romance. As David says, 'Taking off is a risky business, but it is the only way to get anywhere.'

It is vital that we understand our own situations and learn to move on, recognising how the past shapes us without letting it rule us. David opens up our understanding in a very realistic and practical way. His images are a clue to that. He encourages us to consider plants sending up shoots in the garden, the dangers of being hijacked in a plane, trawling for fish, dealing cards, driving to work: each image is related to a different part of his subject.

Marriage and family life are under a great deal of pressure in our society. We all need help to enable us to enter into the right relationship with the best possible likelihood of its growing and developing in a strong, healthy, happy and fulfilling way. This book makes a real contribution to this process for those who have suffered the hurt and damage of divorce. As David puts it, 'Every relationship is hard work but worth it.'

I am delighted to be able to encourage you to read on.

+ Anthony Hereford

Preface

In 1971 I met the girl who would become my wife. We were both members of our church youth club and at that time we were just casual acquaintances. In 1977 we met again, became a couple and four years later we married, by which time I had been ordained in the Church of England for nearly two years. Our marriage lasted seventeen years and then I found myself the lone parent of our four teenage children. I felt as if part of my inner core had been ripped away and I spent the best part of a year with a counsellor – and during this time I initiated divorce proceedings. On our wedding day in 1981 we were surrounded by friends and family; when the marriage ended and my decree absolute arrived in the autumn of 2000, it was without ceremony in the morning post.

Six months later, I started to go out with an old friend – a divorcee herself and the mother of four children. After several months the relationship ended and I hoped that I would meet 'someone', but as the months went by I found myself asking, 'How do I, as a middle-aged parent with commitments coming out of my ears, meet someone else?' Talking this over with a friend, he introduced me to **friends**first, a Christian intro-duction agency. Early on, Gill made contact with me; our friendship blossomed and we married at the end of 2004 – and the rest of our story is on the **friends**first website.

As a member of **friends**first, I talked to the founder,

5

Katharine Gray, on several occasions about my experiences of contacting and meeting **friends**first members. After the publication of my book *Marriage: Restoring Our Vision*, Katharine and I continued to discuss the issues which accompany new friendships – particularly those which arise for the many people who are, like me, divorced.

My personal experience of being a divorcee is not unique. As a vicar I meet many others who find that a new relationship brings joys but raises issues. In the autumn of 2005 Katharine approached me to write this book for members of her agency, recognising that my insights into the 'relationships after divorce' dynamic would be valued by others in the same position.

Since my ordination some twenty-seven years ago, I've married approximately three hundred couples – some of whom were previously divorced. I have also received the confidences of men and women of all ages who were being torn apart as their marriages failed. This book comes out of this crucible of marriage, divorce and remarriage – my own included.

It's a resource for anyone dealing with the reality of making new friends and dating after divorce, and if anything in this Preface sounds familiar, then this book is for you.

Introduction

Very few people take their separation or divorce lightly. For most of us it is an incredibly painful experience which takes time and work to emerge from – at a time when even the smallest tasks seem beyond us. To get through a marriage break-up we need real people to help us (not books!). Friends, family, our church and professional counsellors can help us to come to terms with what has happened. This process is complex because, when we marry, we become one flesh with our spouse and the relationship grows in every part of our lives. When we divorce, tendrils of the marriage still exist and we never completely 'root out' the relationship. As divorcees, we become like gardeners who have rooted out the central plant – but shoots of it keep appearing elsewhere in the garden.

This book is not a counselling manual. In these pages the assumption is that every reader has already done the work necessary to move on from their previous marriage and is ready to make new friendships. Neither does this book explore the rights and wrongs of divorce or remarriage – again, the assumption is that every reader will already have considered the morality of their particular situation. Here the focus is on the unexpected issues which surface once we begin to make those new relationships – because no matter how 'sorted out' we feel about our previous marriage, new friendships not only introduce new issues, they also reintroduce old ones.

If we are aware of these issues and understand why they appear, we are better placed to deal with them – nipping them in the bud and moving forward constructively. If we see the new shoots clearly at an early stage, then we shall have a better idea of how to deal with what may be happening to us.

Who this book is for

This book is a resource for anyone who is:

- divorced and feels sorted out about the past, but unsure about what a fresh start will mean;
- divorced but not sure if they are ready to meet someone new, even though they'd like to;
- divorced and dating, but discovering that they are not as ready as they thought they were;
- dating a divorcee and seeking some insight;
- concerned on behalf of a friend or family member;
- a mixture of several (or all) of the above!

The book is written in three parts

Part 1 considers the impact of a previous marriage and the emotional consequences of divorce. This may feel like going over old ground but the truth is that unless we keep checking, the old shoots grow up all over again. Whether we like it or not, the past sends tendrils into the present and unless we are prepared to deal with them, they will choke off the future.

Part 2 looks at what happens to us when we develop new friendships. This engages our emotions and we probably hope that a personal relationship (an area of life which has lain fallow since the break-up of our marriage) will blossom once more. Wonderful new growth, however, can be accompanied by unwanted shoots from the past, and to make a success of new friendships we have to learn how to disentangle the two.

Part 3 looks at how a new relationship affects those around us. Our friends, family and especially our children (if we have them) are connected to us – and when we begin to connect with someone else, they all have their own issues to deal with too.

In all three parts, issues are highlighted and questions are posed.

Understanding the jargon

There are four phrases in this book used to distinguish different levels of relationship.

1. *Contact:* means letters, phone calls, emails and also initial meetings or 'first dates'.
2. *Dating:* means arranged meetings between people who have already established that they like each other – which may become 'going out' and then 'courting'.
3. *Courting:* means establishing an exclusive relationship where a couple explore their love for one another.
4. *Marriage:* means a committed, lifelong relationship in every sense.

Although in reality these 'levels' of relationship overlap, in this book, generally speaking, the word 'friendship' refers to what's going on in levels 1 or 2 and the word 'relationship' refers to levels 3 or 4.

The aim of this book

The intention is to help everyone recognise common experiences, identify the unexpected and make the most of potential relationships. Whether this book is read from cover to cover, or just dipped into, the aim is to enable those who read it to move into a happy and fulfilling future.

PART 1

WHEN WE DIVORCE

Human beings are not computers, and when things go wrong we cannot just delete unpleasant experiences. Our life story is handwritten, and each day is like a page describing our journey from birth to death. Our past is just as real to us as our present, and both contribute to our future.

We can try, if we want to, to ignore our past. This can appear to be a tempting option – especially when the past is painful – but when we do this, our lives become like stories with missing pages and we stop making sense to ourselves and to others.

In the first part of this book I want to think about the past. We cannot change it – but can we come to terms and live harmoniously with it? Is coming to terms with the past a 'one-off' process or the work of a lifetime? If we are honest about the past, how does this impact on our future?

1

Bereavement

The emotions surrounding divorce are closely related to those surrounding bereavement, because both are experiences of loss. Having said that though, no two bereavements are the same because losing a baby, for example, is not like losing an elderly aunt, which in turn is different from losing a spouse or a parent. Similarly, every divorce is different because it is personal to particular people and circumstances. Also, one partner may feel optimistic about the end of the marriage – while the other partner is devastated. Whatever the circumstances though, and whoever instigates the separation, divorce is nearly always as painful as bereavement.

When we experience loss, one of the most fatuous things that anyone can tell us is that: 'Time is a great healer'. Time in itself achieves nothing, and there are people who, decades after their bereavement or divorce, are still consumed by it. Therefore, what we do with time matters very much, and the priority is to disentangle the death from the funeral or the divorce from the marriage break-up. In the same way that a funeral follows a death but does not cause it, a divorce follows the break-up of a marriage but doesn't really exist in its own right. When we divorce, there are five elements to the experience:

- the pre-marital relationship;
- married life;

- the break-up of the marriage;
- the divorce;
- life after divorce.

It's easy to slip into thinking of the past as a single experience, but the five elements are distinct and we make life doubly hard for ourselves when we allow our emotions about one aspect of what we have been through to bleed into the other four. For example, if we attach current, negative feelings about the divorce to vaguely remembered doubts in the pre-marital relationship the result may be that we re-invent history and blame ourselves, or our ex-spouse unrealistically. This is like looking back with myopic hindsight. Unless we can disentangle the five elements and recognise the positives as well as the negatives in each one, we may become overwhelmed by emotional circularity – which tends to lead to feelings of defeat and a desire to hide behind introversion, escapism or extro-version.

A marriage break-up, like a bereavement, has several phases:

1. denial
2. overwhelming grief
3. emptiness and desolation
4. painful recognition that life goes on
5. life from now on.

Time in itself may not heal anyone, but it is important. No one who loses a loved one can go through the different phases of bereavement in a week; a year or two is usual, although some people get stuck along the way and others spend longer in one phase than another. As divorced people we should recognise the importance of being somewhere in phase 4 or 5 before we begin dating. If we are still locked somewhere in the first three phases, then even if we think that a new relationship will help us through, we are simply not ready. It's vital that we understand this, because if we are not ready to move on from denial, grief or desolation, our experience of making new friends will probably be negative (for both ourselves and the new people we meet) and we may then end up feeling depressed and hopeless – worse off than before!

No, the only way to get to phases 4 and 5 is to go through phases 1 to 3. Until we have done this, we are just not ready for new relationships.

Admitting the pain

The flip-side of the coin of love is bereavement. As divorcees we experience a particular version of this (and if we feel deeply wounded by our ex-spouse, every time we have dealings with them can feel like rubbing salt into that wound). The pain cannot be ignored but friends, church, counselling and our extended family can help us to come to terms with it. The bereavement, though, will always be with us – it's just that if we use the time wisely, after two, five, ten (and so on) years, it will not continually overwhelm us.

We should remember that single people can also be bereaved (of a marriage that never was; of children that never were and so on). None of us has a choice about past pain – it's present whether we acknowledge it or not. The only choice we have is whether to accept it or deny it, and the first step to living in the present is to admit to the pain of the past.

Bearing the pain

Let's think about past pain as a weight. In the first three phases of bereavement, it tends to immobilise us and the length of counselling sessions can be counted in used tissues! At this stage our past pain may feel impossibly heavy and we may think that we shall never be able to carry it around. If we keep lifting it though, and we are guided wisely, we develop new emotional muscles which enable us to carry more weight than we ever imagined possible. Our counsellor, however, cannot carry our pain for us – we have to learn to carry it alone. That's why most successful counselling is through 'professionals' rather than through friends or family.

Those who love us hate our pain and because they have a personal relationship with us they are tempted to try and bear it for us. This is in fact a disservice because it stops us developing the necessary 'emotional muscles' and, ultimately, their love can keep us unhelpfully dependent on them and stuck in the first three phases. Professionals, by comparison, may empathise with us, but they will not attempt to do what only we can do for ourselves. The relationship is not 'personal' and so they are able to make demands of us – even when it hurts!

There is a paradox here which needs to be understood. In a personal relationship, we carry one another's burdens – which means that we ease the load for our friend, and they, in turn, ease ours. When we are in the first three phases of bereavement, however, we may be tempted to embark on a personal relationship – thinking that the other person will carry our pain for us. This just doesn't work, and if we try to do this we may cripple the other person with our needs while refusing to carry a burden which only we can bear. What we need is a 'professional relationship' with someone who can guide us through the first three phases of bereavement.

The principle is this: only when we can carry our past by ourselves, and are in phase 4 or 5 of the bereavement process, are we ready to share the present in a personal relationship.

We are ready to move on when:

- we don't expect another person to wave a magic wand and make our pain go away;

- we appreciate that *we* don't have a magic wand either (to wave over someone else's pain);
- we are able to carry our past and our pain alone;
- we are able to carry the pain of another person and allow them to carry ours.

Living with the pain

Pain can make us either hard or strong but the two are not the same. When pain makes us *hard*, we armour ourselves against future hurt. When pain makes us *strong*, we are able to endure more pain if necessary. When we admit to past pain we become strong and, paradoxically, once we are able to carry our own pain we have arrived at a point where we can share it properly with others. We are then ready for new friendships, dating and new relationships.

Some questions to think about

1. In what ways was my divorce like a bereavement?
2. In what ways was it different?
3. What happens in the present when I retreat into the past?
4. Which phase of bereavement am I really in?
5. What am I expecting from new friends and new relationships *vis-à-vis* my divorce?

2

---◆---

Leaving the past

Even when we have moved through the different phases of bereavement, we still, from time to time, revisit the early stages. This happens when we are overwhelmed by a past memory and allow it to suffocate the present.

Howling at the moon

Most divorced people know this feeling. It can arrive at any time – when we are watching a film, out with friends, enjoying some comfort food, in a business meeting – suddenly, a memory is triggered and we are transported back to that desolate place where we are howling wordlessly. As time goes by, we no longer rush from the room with a mumbled 'Excuse me …'; we just allow the inner, silent wolf its howl.

When we do this, we behave like the wolf who howls to gather the pack. We turn inwards, longing to gather others around our needs. The trouble is – no one else can hear the silent howl, and unless the people we are with know us very well (or are exceptionally perceptive) the message they receive is that we want to be alone. The inner howl is then counter-productive because instead of gathering caring people around us we drive them away. If we can admit to what is happening, it makes it easier to bear, because explaining (with a wry smile) that we've just been overwhelmed by a memory will be understood by most people – especially if we assure them that we'll be fine in a minute.

Once we begin dating, we may find that these 'howling moments' arrive more frequently. This is because we are experiencing intimacy again, and this opens all sorts of doors into the past. It is better to explain to our date why we've suddenly gone quiet, because if we leave them to guess, they'll assume it's because we don't like them. If we are honest, and they like us, they'll understand.

Getting your own back

Telling a new friend about our past is one thing; attempting to enlist their disapproval of our ex-spouse is quite another. If we find ourselves doing this, we are behaving as if there is a raging battle between ourselves and our spouse and we need reinforcements! Instead of building for the future we are, in effect, using the present friendship to bomb the past relationship – which is regress, not progress!

Making friends is an intimate process, and it may stimulate feelings which trigger this desire to lambast our ex-spouse. If this happens, the honest thing to do is to apologise to our new friend; if they like us, they'll put up with the odd rant – as long as we don't expect them to do more than listen.

Forgiving yourself and others

Until we forgive we are stuck in the past; when we forgive, we let go. If we hold on to wrongs done to us (or by us) we remain anchored in the past. When we forgive, we begin to move on, even though the past will occasionally catch us up and overtake us; forgiveness is always progress.

It is impossible for anyone to go through a divorce without the necessity for forgiveness. Whatever happened, and whoever was to blame, we will need to forgive our ex-spouse, anyone else who was involved and ourselves. This is because we are human, and we would need to be sinless to go through such an experience as pure as the driven snow. We all say and do things which we later regret, and most of us fail to do and say things which we know we should. Forgiveness is vital and there is only one way to do it:

- admit the truth;
- forgive.

It may help to remember that real forgiveness isn't an emotion but a decision. It's not a question of 'feeling like it' but of making up our minds and doing it. Neither is forgiveness always a short, one-off event – it can be a process which takes a very long time. Asking whether you've forgiven … (yourself, your ex-spouse, or the actions of others, etc.) is a flippant question. Asking whether you're in the process of forgiving is nearer to the truth. Forgiveness is usually a course of action that needs to start – and continue.

Accepting forgiveness

This can be as hard as forgiving. When we reject the forgiveness of others though, we chain ourselves to the past. We will not let it go, and we keep jabbing ourselves with what we did to see if it still hurts. The moment we accept forgiveness, we leave the past where it is and begin to move on. We remember how hurtful our words or actions were, but we accept the forgiveness of those whom we wronged.

The most common reason for not accepting forgiveness is self-justification (if we convince ourselves that we did nothing wrong, we don't need forgiveness). When this happens, we find that we cannot move on from the past; the only way to make progress is to admit our guilt.

Once we begin to make new friends, our past words and actions may sharpen into new focus. If this prompts us to rethink our behaviour in our previous marriage, we may need to seek the forgiveness of our ex-spouse. Similarly, as a new relationship develops, we need to be honest about our past failings – which means telling our new friend the truth about what we did, and (quite possibly) asking for their forgiveness too. If we are dishonest about our past, how can they trust us in the present or in the future?

Moving on

Guilty or innocent, our past shapes us – we can't ignore it; but we can be shaped positively by it. If we are wise, each time a memory overwhelms us, we engage in actively forgiving and accepting forgiveness yet again. In this way, we keep dealing with the past, and we keep moving on.

Some questions to think about

1. What happens when the past overwhelms the present?
2. Have I begun the process of forgiving those involved in my divorce?
3. Have I begun to forgive myself?

3

Dealing with the past

When the past hijacks the present

Our history is part of who we are, so difficult and painful memories remain with us even when we learn to deal with them. How forceful their presence is depends on us, however. When tragedy strikes, we can think of nothing else. Fifty years later, we may go for years without even thinking about the event, but from time to time we do, and it still has the power to overwhelm us. Past tragedies are like terrorists travelling incognito on a plane. We can be travelling along quite happily, having forgotten that they may be there, but then a place, a smell, a conversation (anything really) triggers a memory, and before we know it we have a hijacker in the cockpit and it's as if we are reliving the tragedy all over again!

When the personal tragedy is a marriage break-up, anyone who asks 'Are you over your divorce?' doesn't understand human beings. To be 'over' a divorce would mean somehow expunging from our history not only the break-up, but the marriage itself (and the courting which led to it) – all of which contribute to who we are. Our past relationship may be over, but it continues to shape our present.

Identifying the terrorist

As divorced people, we may be cautious about potential relationships with other divorcees. We may feel that two terrorist factions in one plane are more than we can handle – but we tend to forget that everyone has terrorists! A person who has been single for many years may carry personal tragedies from their past – for example, they may be deeply wounded that they never married, or that they never had children. They may be injured by a courtship which came to nothing or by the constant nagging of their extended family. A single person may well have as many terrorists as a divorced person – it's just that their hijackers are different!

When we first pluck up enough courage to try and make contact with new people we may feel devastated when some of them reject us because we are divorced. We must understand that they are just frightened of our past and how it affects our present, not of us.

There is only one way to deal with the past; accept it and learn to recognise a hijack. When the past intrudes, it will seek to reset our course, and if we are not ready for this we fall in with the hijacker's demands. For example, perhaps in our previous marriage (or during the divorce) we developed feelings of aggression, inadequacy or self-pity. Now that we are making new friends we are feeling positive, generous and giving – until a memory is triggered and we find ourselves being spiteful, desperate and needy. We thought we were on course for a new destination, but now we feel as if we are right back where we started – the hijack has been a total success!

In a real plane, with real terrorists, the only way to survive is to capitulate by accepting their demands. In life, when the metaphorical terrorists arrive, we can accept them, be sad about the past, but refuse to change course. It may take a little time (and we may need some time by ourselves to recover) but these 'terrorists' will slink back to their seats again – until next time.

The possibilities for the future

To continue the image of flying, the only safe place is on the ground! When it comes to people though, relationships are never 'safe', because they involve trusting someone else. If we stay on the ground, we play safe and lose. Taking off is a risky business, but it's the only way to get anywhere.

As we get to know another person, we can learn to identify their terrorists as they learn to recognise ours. We can help them through each attack just as they can help us when we are being assaulted. If we think that we shall meet someone without personal terrorists we are crazy; if they have a past, they will have terrorists, just as we do. A successful relationship consists of two people who love each other enough to deal with each other's pasts – not of two people who have no pasts to deal with.

Some questions to think about

1. Have I experienced the past hijacking the present?
2. What do I want someone to be for me?
3. What do I want to be for them?

PART 2

WHEN WE DEVELOP NEW FRIENDSHIPS

We've recognised that the past is important. It shapes us, but it should not rule us. Even though the past occasionally hijacks the present, if we understand what is happening, and learn how to deal with it, we are ready to move on. This is particularly true for relationships.

When we begin to make new friendships, a number of issues will inevitably arise. It may seem like hard work to face these issues, but they can be thought of as important building blocks in the new relationship. Addressing these issues is like lifting the blocks and placing them appropriately in order to build securely, and strongly, for the future.

4

Plenty more fish in the sea

By making new friends, we are being proactive about the rest of our lives. Once we begin to make contact with others though, we soon realise that they are being proactive too. Understanding our own past and our own pain is a good education because it helps us to understand, and be kind to, other people – because they too have a past.

We have the rest of our life ahead of us; our divorce is behind us and now we want to make a new relationship – a prospect which may make us both nervous and excited. Perhaps friends and relations are assuring us that there are plenty more fish in the sea, but is this really true?

Taking stock

We are who we are, and our past is what it is. If we are going to make any meaningful relationships in the future we must start right here (not back where we were before our previous marriage). For example, at forty-nine years of age and divorced after a thirty-year marriage, it's as impossible to return emotionally to the age of nineteen as it is to cram a middle-aged body into trendy clothes and become a teenager once more.

So, starting here, what do we actually want from the social contacts we are making? Passionate romance? Gentle

31

companionship? Security? Excitement? What? It's worth sitting down with a piece of paper, and writing two headings: 'What I was looking for then' and 'What I am looking for now'. Try and think back – and spend some time making a list which answers the first question. Then, move on to the second. Comparing the two lists may help to clarify what we want now, and why. It may also enable us to relate to new people, and develop new relationships, in a way which is appropriate to us now.

A word to the men

Ok guys, here's the truth. Men fancy young women – but if we are sixty years of age, unless we are an ageing rock-star or a millionaire, no woman of twenty-five is likely to date us. If we *are* an ageing rock-star or a millionaire, then we might well join an introduction agency precisely to avoid the kind of twenty-five-year-old woman who's currently interested in us!

Seriously, age matters. Once the age difference widens to more than a decade or so, we flirt with the generation gap. Men might like the bodies of younger women, but unless we have frittered away our years, our conversation and attitudes to life will be different. A much younger woman won't help an older man to recapture his lost youth, for it's just that: already lost.

Being realistic

The older we get the more we have invested in our lives. When we first leave home as young adults, we may begin with little more than a few boxes full of personal possessions and a readiness to set up home anywhere. As the decades roll by though, we have jobs, mortgages and houses full of contents which would take tens of thousands of pounds to replace. More significantly, we may have invested years in our community, our job, our network of friends, and so forth. We may also have made sacrifices in order to be near our extended family.

If we make a successful new relationship, it may be with someone who wants to move their own life lock, stock and barrel into ours, but what if they want us to move a hundred per cent into theirs? Are we ready to reinvest somewhere else? If we are realistic about who we are and what can be, we are in a better position to make proper choices about the future.

Weighing up

A new relationship will be costly because the flame of passion requires more fuel than just love – it needs self-sacrifice, time, energy and money. At its most basic level, a dinner date requires a free evening (with childcare arrangements when children are part of the equation), a journey and payment of the restaurant bill. As a relationship develops, the time commitment escalates – and so does the financial cost.

These material costs are mirrored by the spiritual and emotional costs. As divorcees, we have experienced marriage and know the various bills that must be paid. For us though, there is a hidden 'service charge' called trust. As our previous relationship developed, we probably gave our trust without thinking about it. Now that our trust has been betrayed (or now that we have betrayed that trust) we find it much more difficult to trust all over again. For a relationship to be healthy though, trust needs to be mutual; we need to learn to trust again because then we, in turn, can be trusted.

Finding a new fish

Are there plenty more fish in the sea? Yes, but the ocean's a big place, lots of fish are already committed, and we need to find an available fish we are compatible with. When we first 'trawled' for a partner, our options may have been very wide, but because our history shapes us, we may now find that our options are more limited. In our society, joining an introduction agency is one way of making contact with available fish. Sticking with that agency is about being realistic – we may need to meet a significant part of the shoal before we recognise a kindred sole ... er ... soul.

Some questions to think about

1. Am I ready to trust again?
2. Am I being realistic about who I want to meet?

5

Making contact

Our society is geared towards individuality – which is a problem, because individuals tend to be footloose and fancy-free. We have lost our sense of community, and although some 'neighbourhoods' still exist, most people 'network'. In other words, we work, shop, socialise and worship away from home. This means that our friends tend to live at a distance, and when it comes to meeting new friends it's hard to know where to start.

One way to meet new friends is to join an 'interest group'. If we like drama or art or sport, then joining a club of like-minded people helps us to meet others. As we drive to this new club of twenty people though, we may pass several hundred other people all driving to their own respective interest groups. Perhaps we would get on with some of them really well – but we shall never know because we have no way of meeting them.

Increasingly, dating agencies and friendship agencies offer a way of making contact with people who we would otherwise not meet. Some agencies take on the responsibility of 'pairing' people for a date; other agencies distribute information and allow members to decide for themselves. **friends**first is one such agency where personal profiles are distributed widely, and members are actively encouraged and supported to make contact with each other by letter, phone or email.

Initial contact is a gentle way of establishing whether we

want to meet one another. Let's be honest with ourselves – receiving a letter or a phone call is deliciously exciting, but initiating the contact is nerve-racking. When we are contacted, we can shape our response accordingly; when we initiate the contact, we have to expose more of ourselves. In the end though, however we do this, and whoever makes the first contact, until we actually meet we are always at a distance. Unless we have joined an introduction agency to enlarge our circle of pen-friends, sooner or later we must meet.

Mind the gap!

It is only by meeting that we really get to know one another. This is when we read the body language and the hundreds of subtle facial expressions and tones of voice which tell us what we need to know. Until we meet, every letter and phone call has gaps – and if we are not careful, we fill these with our imagination. Email can be particularly prone to this because it is immediate and if we give the words on the screen an imaginary face and voice we end up with interactive fiction.

Divorced people are especially predisposed to this because we are used to intimacy, and contact feels intimate. If we make good contacts, but are disappointed when we meet those contacts in the flesh, the problem is probably our own imagination and the way in which we 'filled the gaps' in letters, emails or phone calls.

Serious or fun?

Joining a friendship agency like **friends**first gives us the chance to make contacts; the rest is up to us. Perhaps it helps to remember those four social levels of relationship outlined earlier:

- *Contact* (letters, phone calls and emails). These are exciting contacts which brighten our day.
- *Dating* (arranged meetings). These are enjoyable opportunities to get to know new people.
- *Courting* (establishing an exclusive relationship). This is serious because we are finding out if we have a future together.
- *Marriage* (a committed relationship). This is as serious as it can get because now we give ourselves to each other.

Contact is neither courting nor marriage, and neither is dating. Most people have no idea from a first contact where it will lead, which is why **friends**first, for example, encourages members to contact as many people as possible. The same is true of dating, and the best way to make meetings fun is to understand the different levels.

As people who have been previously married, we have probably spent our marriage determinedly not flirting with anyone other than our spouse. Now, when making new friendships, we may feel uncomfortable about it. If we appreciate that flirting can be 'level-1' behaviour, we can even practise it in daily life (with shop assistants, bus drivers, and all those fleeting strangers we meet). If we are never going to meet these people again, we are not giving them the 'come on'; we're just brightening their day, and sharpening up a skill which has gone blunt, so that we can use it appropriately in 'level-2' situations to signal the way we feel.

Expectations

At a first meeting (which may, or may not, be a first date), we all want to show ourselves in our best light. The clothes we wear are important, but friendship is more than skin deep. Maybe we have bought a new wardrobe, lost weight, switched to contact lenses and availed ourselves of all the 'look young and sexy' products on the market. We are still ourselves though, aren't we?

In the process of getting ready to date, TV programmes can help. Tips on what to wear and what suits our physique and colouring are very valuable. So are the programmes which teach ordinary people how to flirt. They are tips however, not biblical commandments, and we must think of clothes as packaging and flirting as advertising. Ultimately, they are either honest or dishonest, depending on the product (on this occasion, us!).

As divorced people, we may need to think about our clothes and the way we behave with the opposite sex. As a result of the divorce, we may want to change our image completely – but if our new image doesn't reflect who we are, then we become like a big exciting package which contains a disappointing product!

It's far better to start where we are and develop what we have. We are not so much 'starting again' as 'starting the rest of our life' and we should begin by expecting the best for ourselves. Our date will pick up on this.

Spouse mark 2

Our divorce may have hurt and damaged us, but it will not necessarily have changed us. We are the same person we always were, just an injured version. Even when the wounds have healed, the flesh and blood beneath is still intrinsically 'us'. Amongst other things, this will mean that our 'type' (what we look for in the opposite sex) has probably not changed. This is because we get on with people who are both:

- similar enough to us to be comfortable;
- different enough from us to be interesting.

38

Human beings are complex, and not everyone marries their 'type'. If this applies to us, then as divorcees we may be jubilant that now we can look for 'our type'. We may need to recognise though that we married our first spouse (even if they weren't our type) because we are who we are. We may find that, second time around, we again end up courting a 'type' similar to our ex-spouse!

Whether we look for a similar or dissimilar 'type' to our previous spouse, we should recognise that every human being is an individual. Therefore, even though the vast majority of second spouses 'resemble' the first, this doesn't predestine the second marriage to failure. Type is like nationality; each 'type' contains millions of individuals. At levels 1 and 2 (contact and dating) we need to resist the impulse to 'decide the future' based on whether this person is 'just like' or 'completely different from' our ex-spouse. The only way to find out what the future holds is to get to know this person as an individual.

At contact and dating levels, there are only two relevant questions:

1. Do I like this person?
2. Does this person like me?

Real priorities

Once we start making contact, and particularly when we begin to meet new people and date, we shouldn't be surprised that certain personal issues surface.

- We may begin to recognise ourselves. Here are we, chatting with someone new, but – hang on a minute – we sound just like we did when we chatted to our spouse. At this point we realise that we haven't fundamentally changed – we are still ourselves. This is normal, and an important truth – if we don't learn it, we pretend to be what we are not.

- All this attention is delightful. Here we are, and it feels intimate. Wait though, what if this person is lying, leading us on, getting ready to hurt us? At this point we discover that our healed wounds have scars.
- What if this person is 'the one'? We have come to terms with our new life and got used to making our own decisions. What will a new relationship replace? Maybe we've made our job the focus of our life (or our home, our children, our church or our leisure interests) – but this person will turn all of that upside down, because if we get serious this person will become our first priority, and we shall become theirs.

And now we understand. At the age of twenty, meeting someone is like playing 'snap'; there are only two people involved. After divorce at any age, meeting someone is more like trying to shuffle two packs of cards together. It begins to dawn on us that this might not be as easy as we imagined – which is, of course, why you are reading this book!

Some questions to think about

1. Why am I seeking to meet a significant other? What do I really want?
2. Am I looking for someone similar to my ex, or someone completely different? Why?
3. When I meet new people, do I compare them with my ex? Or do I check them against a 'perfect person' list in my head? Or do I just get to know them?

6

---◄○►---

Falling in love again

So, we have made contact, been dating, and now we are courting. Thus far, we have been having fun together and doing some serious thinking. Now we are getting serious about each other and the fun contributes building blocks to our relationship. This new relationship might end in marriage, so let's ask a question: 'Is love all we need?' The true answer is: 'It depends on what you mean by love.'

Love, friendship and lust

First-century Greeks (sensible people) used four different words for love:

- *Philein* meant to love as a sibling, desiring the best for another.
- *Eran* meant erotic love (this word is the root of 'erotic').
- *Agapan* meant the self-giving, self-sacrificial love that gives all and expects nothing in return. (This is the word most often used by Christian writers to express God's love for humanity.)
- *Storge* meant the love of a parent for a child.

We, in our culture, confuse the four and often mistake them

for each other. Although there are occasions when husband and wife 'baby' each other, *storge* does not primarily belong to an adult relationship, so we'll focus on the other three.

In our society, many relationships rely heavily on *eran*. We are surrounded by bodies, erotica and sex. Marriages based on *eran* though, tend to fail because looks change and fade. More importantly, *eran* doesn't engender either *philein* or *agapan*; it tends to take what it wants and leave.

Philein, however, is the foundation of friendship. It can stimulate both *eran* and *agapan*, which is why people who on first meeting are not attracted to each other may become lovers after making friends. In a marriage, we commit to each other whatever the future will bring. Who knows – perhaps prostate problems and gynaecological procedures will make *eran* impossible? When a couple are friends first and foremost, they will be friends last too – and where there is *agapan* that friendship will last to the end.

Agapan summarises Christian marriage vows – where the expectation is that we will give ourselves to each other and place the needs of our spouse above our own. As divorced people, it helps us to identify which 'loves' were present in our previous marriage, and in what order. When we are courting again, the Greeks can help us to figure out what's going on with our new 'love'. We may also discover sensitive areas in our past (and present) where we are fragile or deluded. Now is the time to test our new relationship with honesty; if it has a future, then we must trust our shortcomings to our partner. If they have *philein* and *agapan* for us, then the relationship will deepen. If they do not, well, we've found out now and the courtship has been a success. Discovering that we are not right for each other is as important as finding out that we are.

Loving our ex-spouse

Once we understand that there are four 'loves' it becomes possible to love our ex-spouse appropriately. We can express *philein* by making the divorce settlement fair, being reasonable about family matters and establishing a beneficial pattern of contact with any children. We are no longer obliged to behave towards our ex with *agapan* because our lives are no longer interconnected. Similarly, we may find that *eran* has withered or (surprisingly) is still present; so what? This just means that we are alive and conscious of gender!

Sometimes, in the divorce relationship, we may need *storge*. Like a parent making decisions about a beloved child, we may need to say 'No' to our ex-spouse, exclude them from the personal details of our life and make hard decisions about their access to us. Basically, we shall need to define emotional, organisational and personal boundaries, and these will probably change over time. If we begin courting, these boundaries may need revisiting and redefining. If the new relationship is serious, then our potential spouse has every right to be part of the process.

Whether such boundary changes are done at a distance through solicitors, or close up through personal discussion, they can still be done lovingly – as long as we understand the four loves, and the differences between them.

Fearing the worst

If getting married was scary and getting divorced was terrifying, any new relationship can similarly be characterised by fear. We may be tempted to cling on instead of give, but to do this is the antithesis of love. Love, in all four aspects, is self-giving. When we cling, we want the best for ourselves; when we love, we want the best for the other person. Two mis-quotations sum up the truth:

1. It's better to have loved and lost than to have clung on and won.
Love involves giving, and to have a relationship there must be mutual love. At some point in their life most people experience love for someone who doesn't love them back, but to manipulate that person into a relationship is unloving and destructive.

2. Perfect fear casts out all love.
Fear is to love what a bucket of water is to a flame. If we fear losing the person we love, we make the loss more likely! The trick is to forget ourselves and to concentrate on the other person – trusting them to do the same.

There is a paradox at the heart of human relationships, because when we take, we lose and when we give we gain. Christians believe that this is because human love mirrors the love of God, but whatever we believe, the result is the same; give love and a relationship grows – try to demand love and watch the relationship wither.

Building relationships which last

After divorce, making new friendships (let alone a new relationship) can be very difficult – unless we understand what we bring to them. If we appreciate the differences between *philein, agapan* and *eran* then we are more likely to establish both friendships and relationships on a sound foundation. If we also understand about giving, then we build securely on that foundation.

Whether we are making contact, dating or courting, it's good to remember: *philia protos* (friendship first!) and to remind ourselves that there is more than one kind of love.

Some questions to think about

1. Were *philein, eran* and *agapan* present in my previous marriage?
2. Does understanding that there are different 'loves' help me to deal with my ex-spouse?
3. Am I a giver or a clinger?
4. Am I cautious of new relationships because I fear commitment?

7

Getting physical

Although our contemporary culture tends to separate sex from love, Christians are generally agreed that this is both wrong and mistaken. In this book we are thinking within a framework of Christian morality, therefore stewarding our sexuality is an important part of every social contact.

When we are young, and first begin to date, it's important to steward our sexual urges so that they parallel both our emotions and commitment. As a relationship deepens, we make choices about 'how far' to go physically, and as each new level begins, there is the thrill of discovery.

When we are married, we settle into a pattern of love-making which suits both partners. Sometimes we experience the highs, sometimes the lows, and, a lot of the time, love-making is ordinary but important. Now that we are divorced, this sexual pattern is in the past, but when we begin to date, it may well emerge into the present.

Dating after divorce

Let's think sideways for a moment and consider the image of driving to work every day. The route becomes second nature because we've done it so often and we don't really think much about it. We may find that we've turned corners and negotiated junctions without even being aware of it. In a marriage, love-making can become just as familiar, and an initial kiss, or holding hands, almost inconsequential.

Now, however, we are divorced and on a date with someone new. Though to us a kiss at the end of the evening may be no more important than casually saying 'Goodnight', the person we are kissing may think differently – that kiss, for them, may be tantamount to a confession of undying love! Similarly, if we embark on a new relationship, we may be so excited by this rekindled physicality that we find ourselves travelling down that oh so familiar route – without really thinking about it.

This tendency to go 'too far too quickly' is an issue for divorced people. If we understand it, we are prepared for it, and so do not allow our bodies to express a commitment we are not emotionally ready to make.

Different expectations

As we explore a new relationship, it's important to be clear about our future expectations of each other. It's very common to assume that young couples have similar sexual expectations of their partner, but this may not be true, and as we grow older it's even more important to sort out our expectations. A mature couple will experience significant problems if one person is looking for a marriage which will mean purely companionship and the other is expecting a full sexual relationship.

It's probably unwise to ask another person about their sexual intentions on first contact – or even on an early date! On the other hand, the more friendly we become the more likely we are to assume that we know what they are thinking. Therefore, whatever our age, the rule is this: communication. Stop imagining (or stop kissing) and start talking.

Establishing a new pattern

As divorced people, we need to be clear about one thing. We can never go back; we can only begin the rest of our life – in every way, including sexually.

When we are divorced or bereaved, our bed can feel very empty and cold. We may be tempted to fill it with 'any body' but this is false comfort because every 'body' is a person. Sex and relationships are inextricably bound together and although the mechanics of sex are pretty similar regardless of the person, every relationship is different. Therefore an appropriate, new sexual pattern will not depend on physical practices, but upon the relationship two people build together.

As divorced people, we build for the future when we shrug off the familiar sexual pattern belonging to our previous marriage and concentrate on the new relationship. While dating and courting, identifying mutual 'boundaries' helps – and sticking to them helps even more! Linking the sexual journey to the level of commitment isn't just a sensible precaution – it ensures that we can end an inappropriate relationship as easily as we can develop an appropriate one, because we only allow our bodies to commit to what we are emotionally ready for.

Some questions to think about

1. When dating or courting, do I find it difficult to steward my sex-drive? Why?
2. If a relationship develops beyond the dating phase, at what point shall we know one another's sexual expectations for this relationship?

8

Going public

Divorce has a habit of tearing down our boundaries, like a tank crashing through every defence between us and the outside world. Emotionally, we tend to lose our sense of perspective and either keep everyone beyond the outer perimeter, or let everyone into our most personal thoughts and feelings. When we do this we become either the person who never reveals anything personal to anyone, or the person who emotionally strips to strangers. In the process of meeting new people it's as much of a disaster to bare all after five minutes as it is to share nothing after fifty years! Once we begin to meet new people, we shall need to 'manage' our boundaries.

It helps to imagine that we are surrounded by a series of concentric circles. Each circle is a 'fence', and each fence has its own gate which is 'information'. If we chat to a stranger, we may allow them through 'gate 1' into our outer circle. We may allow our best friend all the way in – or we may reserve the last gate (or two) for our spouse.

When we make contact, date, court and marry, different levels of access are appropriate. Therefore it's useful to consider our contact and dating boundaries, but the issue is wider – how much do we tell our children, our friends or our extended family?

With each other

When we meet new people, it's right to maintain our 'fences'. This is not dishonest; it's just a question of appropriate access. Honesty is about telling the truth – it doesn't mean telling everything all at once. Revealing too much, too soon, can be a manipulative and abusive way of seizing or giving away control.

As divorced people, this may take a little getting used to. We are used to our spouse having access to our innermost self; re-establishing the fences may take time and practice.

We can all use information to manipulate. Knowledge, as we all know, is power. An abiding characteristic of love though, in any of its four forms, is honesty.

With children

If we have children and they live with us after the divorce, we may be tempted to re-evaluate their level of access. Instead of keeping them safely inside (let's say) fence four, we open up to them in a more personal way. In short, instead of parenting them, we make them our friends, or worse still, a sort of surrogate spouse. We tell them things they don't need to know, and to alleviate our loneliness, we burden them.

What we tell our children matters, because it signifies our relationship with them. What we tell small children, teenagers or grown-up children will be different, but the principle still applies – we are their parents, not their friends or partners.

A large part of parenting is example. Therefore, if we tell lies about dating (as in: 'Bye dear, I'm off to my pottery class again') so will they. We must be honest about meeting new people, but at an appropriate information level. If this provokes a negative response we just have to deal with the fallout – after all, this is part of parenting too.

With an ex-spouse

Now that we are divorced, we shall have to decide on the level of access our ex-spouse has to our life. This is complicated, because until our separation they had access to our innermost selves. Since then though, our lives have diverged, and they do not have automatic access to anything. We must choose what information to share, and at what level.

With our extended family

When we divorce, our extended family may take sides. If our parents, uncles, cousins and so forth see us as the victim, they can be inappropriately enthusiastic when we meet someone new. Similarly, if they blame us for the divorce, they can be inappropriately critical of any new friend.

It's right to look for the approval of our extended family, because they know us well. After divorce though, things can get complicated. At the very least, we should be honest with our new friend about why our extended family hold their views, and, where possible, we should encourage contact. If the relationship develops into a marriage, our extended family is usually part of the deal.

Some questions to think about

1. Are my 'information fences' in good order? Do I manage my personal boundaries well?
2. Who will I tell about my new contacts?
3. At what point will I tell my children (if I have them) or my ex-spouse?

9

Building on quicksand

When we make contact with another person there are two questions to ask: (1) 'Do I want to meet this person?' and (2) 'Do they want to meet me?' After meeting them and discovering whether we like each other (see Chapter 5) there is another question to ask: (3) 'Are we going to meet again?' If we begin courting, then we are finding out if we love each other. After a while we may conclude that we are not compatible (even if we love each other) and decide to end the relationship. Or, we begin to ask a fourth question: (4) 'Do I want to marry this person?'

If the relationship is to succeed, the answer to any of these questions will be nothing to do with showing off, revenge or selfishness. Being human though, and especially when we carry unacknowledged issues from our past, sometimes we reject the solid foundations upon which a long-term relationship can be built and play power games instead. If we descend into this kind of behaviour (which can be all too easy) we might 'win' a few games, but in the long term we lose – because a new relationship is then built on a foundation of quicksand.

Every relationship is either a balance of power or a balance of empowering. When a marriage is going well there will be mutual empowerment, but during a divorce, couples may exchange this for wielding power over one another. Most usually, the ammunition will be finances, any children involved and new relationships.

Showing off

We can use our dates as a means of showing off to our ex-spouse, friends, church, family and so forth. We will tell ourselves that we are showing everyone that we are 'over' the divorce and that we are still attractive (and find reasons to justify dating the youngest and most lovely people we can).

The truth is that we lack confidence, and are stuck in phase 3 of the bereavement process (feeling empty and desolate). We are in fact using our dates to make us feel better about ourselves. To be frank, we are not really interested in those we're dating; they are just tokens of our health and sex appeal. We should not be surprised if they resent being seen as objects, and leave us flat.

Revenge

When children are hurt they say: 'I'll show them ... I'll show them all!' When we are divorced, we can revert to childhood, and date just to 'show' our ex-spouse. When we do this, we tell ourselves that new relationships will help us to get over our failed marriage. We tend not to care who we date, as long as we have someone. We may also be pulled towards promiscuous behaviour – partly out of a feeling of wanting to make up for lost time, and partly out of a desire to hurt our ex-spouse. We may even want to hurt God.

The truth is that we are deeply hurt and stuck in phase 2 of the bereavement process (overwhelming grief). We are, actually, using our date(s) to take revenge. With any luck, they will leave us to our self-pity; if we are out of luck, they will be using us in the same way (to get back at *their* ex-spouse), and then we're both in real trouble!

ₛ that selfishness is intrinsic to the human
ᵣibutor to our fallen nature. When we justify
ᵣselves, but after divorce, it's easy to slip into
self-ᵃᵤ.   ₊Ne say to ourselves: 'I've had a lousy time … I
deserve …' and if we are the perceived 'victim', our friends and
extended family may agree with us. We should step very
carefully here, because when it comes to a relationship, no one
'deserves' anyone.

If we are heading towards a marriage then it's good to
remember that this is not a reward but a covenant and a
sacrifice. We willingly enter into it because we wish to
empower each other – because we love one another (and to
understand 'love' we should refer to Chapter 6).

Jumping the gun

One personal issue is that if we date before our divorce is
granted, or date a separated person, we attempt to move on
from a previous marriage while at the same time beginning a
new relationship. Most professional counsellors advise against
this because the conflicting emotions can pull us apart.

In practical terms, we should also beware of becoming a
pawn in someone else's legal game. For example, perhaps our
date is presuming that after a two-year separation their divorce
will be a 'no fault' arrangement. Their ex-spouse though,
knows that they are dating us – and in order to gain a better
financial settlement, may decide to cite us as the corespondent
and begin divorce proceedings on the grounds of adultery.
Even if our behaviour has been beyond reproach, unless our
meetings have been chaperoned we shall have a hard time
defending our reputation.

Empowering

Playing power games is a recipe for failure because although power might seem attractive, seductive and exciting, ultimately it corrupts. Our desire for a relationship will need to connect with our desire to empower – which means hard work and personal sacrifice – but ultimately, empowering others is both exciting and life-giving. So in a relationship (and let's have another misquote): 'Ask not what this person can do for you, but what you can do for this person!'

Some questions to think about

1. In what ways am I on the rebound?
2. When I meet new people, how will knowing me benefit them?
3. If I make a friend, will this be enough?
4. Am I using new relationships to play power games?

10

Contemplating remarriage

Different people have different expectations about the future –
but life often delivers the unexpected. Some divorcees
conclude that they will never remarry – only to meet their
future spouse the very next week. Others long to remarry but
never do. The future is partly in our control and partly beyond
our control because although we can help shape the future by
living appropriately in the present and properly handling the
past, we cannot know if we shall experience 'good fortune'. So,
whether we think that we shall remarry or not, by making new
contacts, new friends and new relationships, we are at least
acknowledging the possibility. This means that we should be
prepared to do some thinking about remarriage even if we have
no plans to remarry at the moment.

Being judged by others

Once we are divorced, we discover that different people attach
different moral judgements to us. At one extreme, there are
people who accept divorce whatever the cause; at the other
extreme there are those who regard any divorce as morally
unacceptable. Consequently, as divorcees, in casual
conversations, we have probably learned to hesitate before
revealing our marital status.

We have now left the divorce behind us but if we come to the point of contemplating remarriage, there are new moral rapids to negotiate in the form of four broad categories of opinion:

1. Divorce is always wrong, so remarriage is always wrong.
2. Divorce in certain circumstances is right, but any subsequent remarriage is wrong while the previous spouse is alive.
3. Divorce in certain circumstances is right; therefore the rightness of a remarriage will depend on the reasons for the divorce.
4. Divorce is just a fact, so remarriage is always right.

We need to think carefully about where we stand in relation to these views.

Our own view

We know the details of our own divorce, and the temptation is to spin the facts in our favour. It's more honest though to admit to our own part in the divorce and have a clear understanding of why the marriage failed.

If we are considering a remarriage, we need to be open about the reasons for our divorce. We need also to decide whether it is morally appropriate for us to remarry. Assuming we believe divorce 'in certain circumstances' is right, do our circumstances correspond to those? Simply to say 'I want to get married' is making light of a serious matter. If we don't face this issue honestly then we shall probably retain a nagging feeling that we are being 'unfaithful' to our ex-spouse, regardless of the truth.

Our church's view

If we are a Christian, the opinion of our church will be important to us. It's worth taking some time to sort the question of remarriage out sooner rather than later. Spending two years meeting, dating and courting, and only then ringing the minister's doorbell and announcing 'We'd like to get married – and we'd like you do it!' risks being met with a frosty response.

It's far better to have a conversation with the minister before the dating stage. At the very least we'll know where we stand. If any relationship develops to the point of marriage, we already know the parameters, and the likely framework of moral values our church works within. At best, we'll consider our options with this in mind.

Our church may, however, make it clear to us that it will never endorse any future marriage. We then have some hard thinking to do and perhaps some painful choices to make.

The prospect of remarriage

Some people join friendship agencies for casual companionship, or just to make friends, but many join with the hope that they will marry. Therefore the prospect of marriage may well touch even first contacts. If we are to proceed with integrity we need to show our respect for others by sorting out the morals of divorce and remarriage – in our own minds and with our church – at a very early stage.

Some questions to think about

1. If I meet a potential spouse, how will this relationship change my life?

58

2. What will it mean for my new spouse to share their life with me?

3. Does the prospect of remarriage sit comfortably with my conscience? Would my church approve?

PART 3

HOW A NEW RELATIONSHIP AFFECTS FAMILY LIFE

Every relationship affects us. We may be changed out of all recognition for the better – or altered for the worse. As we begin to make new friends after our divorce, the key for *us* is to understand our previous marriage as well as the break-up. We are not in this alone though.

As well as being an ex-spouse, we are likely to have a number of other close relationships – with parents, siblings, children and so forth. The closer these relations are to us, the more they will be affected by any new relationship we make, and this is particularly true for any children we have.

From the moment we begin dating, children begin to wonder about their future. Even if no new relationship develops into a marriage, our children, siblings and parents all imagine that each one might. This possibility affects children more directly than any other member of our family and so in this section we begin by exploring the issues from their point of view.

11

A child's perspective

As we all know, divorce affects children deeply, and so do new relationships. We cannot change this, but we can understand it and in this way minimise the trauma for them. In this, life is the same for children as it is for adults; they cannot remove past pain, only accept it and deal with it, or deny it.

Their pain

Children are usually deeply wounded by divorce. Their dearest wish is that their parents will stop fighting, make up and get back together. They often feel that the divorce is in some way their fault. They know that both of their parents still love them, but that's not the point; they hate the fact that their parents no longer love each other. When all parents do is assure their children that they are still loved, they put a plaster on the one place where there is no wound.

Children tend not to articulate pain; instead, they express it through their behaviour. A small child is unlikely to scream 'I hate you!' They are more likely to slam the door, again, and again, and again. Because divorce is like bereavement, it may help if our children attend one of the counselling opportunities geared specifically towards them (see p. 79).

A potential step-parent

The relationship between step-parents and step-children is notoriously difficult (just read *Cinderella*!). Children know this and they have probably heard all sorts of horror stories from their friends. From the moment their parents separate they begin to worry about their future family life. Younger children think of a step-parent in terms of a 'new mum or dad' while older children (especially when they are approaching their twenties) tend to regard them as welcome, or unwelcome, equals – much like an extra 'house mate'. This means that as soon as we begin to make new friends, any children involved will immediately begin to size them (or us) up as a potential step-parent.

Two key interfaces between adults and children (of any age) are household chores and discipline, and they will therefore want to find out where any potential step-parent stands in relation to them. Will this new adult want to change everything? Will they be stricter or more lenient than their existing parent?

In order to find answers to their questions, many children will behave close to the edge of their usual boundaries just to see what happens. They may want to know if their parent will side with them or with the new friend. They may try to manipulate the new friend into giving permission for something they know will be denied by their parent. This kind of behaviour isn't 'bad'; what's happening is this – the child doesn't feel able to discuss their concerns with either their parent or the potential step-parent because they feel that any discussion will be one-sided, with the adults holding all the power. Instead, they will 'test' the new relationship to see how it affects them (to see what it would be like to be the child of this potential couple) by the only means available to them – behaviour.

This experience can come as something of a shock. We, as adults, are enjoying a new friendship, but we are nowhere near making a decision about marriage. When we invite our new friend home, we are stunned and embarrassed by the children's behaviour – after all, they are usually as good as gold! The key is this: *we* may not be thinking beyond friendship, but the children are.

A potential new family

Because children think in terms of remarriage (even at the earliest stage of a friendship) they will consider the effect the new relationship might have on their family life. They have survived the upheaval of the divorce, settled into the new 'divorced pattern', and now they are facing another upheaval. Will they have step-siblings? Will their parent have another baby with this new spouse? Do they like this new adult – and does this new adult like them?

From children's point of view, neither step-siblings nor a new baby will in themselves carry either positive or negative values – what matters to them is:

- the stability of their home;
- a secure framework where they know their boundaries;
- being loved.

If children feel threatened by this new friendship, they will resist it in every way they can. If they see the new relationship as a good thing, they will do everything they can to encourage wedding bells.

Once again: the adults may not be thinking beyond friendship, but the children will be. From the very first moment when they meet our new friend, mentally, they will be either booking the church or reaching for a machine gun.

A potentially intimate relationship

One change that children often don't know how to handle is the realisation that their parents have sexual desires. In a family where the parents remain together in their first marriage, children reach an age where they refuse to believe that their parents still make love. When their parents divorce, if either party is with a new partner then they are forced to accept the reality – but they often don't like it. This may have little to do with the morals of the situation – for children it's just the thought of Mum or Dad …doing that!

When adults make new friends and begin to date or court, the children cannot escape the fact that there is more than conversation going on. They may well find the thought of their parent kissing a new friend distasteful (but remember, the idea of their parents kissing each other would be just as distasteful!). What we have to understand is this: their reaction to the potential sexual activity of their parent has little to do with the new relationship – it's just that children don't like to think of their parents in any sexual sense.

Children may take every opportunity to share their views in a tangential way. For example, they may do this by saying aloud 'Yuk! Old people!!!' when a couple on TV are over forty. This is just their way of telling us that they know – and they want us to know that they know. We don't need to respond, argue, ridicule or organise a formal debate. All we need to do is let them know that we *know* that they know.

Power games

Small children display their emotions physically; older children tend to do so 'emotionally'. They still may not talk about their feelings – instead they go quiet, storm out, cultivate dumb insolence, manipulate arguments (and a hundred other emotional behaviours). In short, they begin to explore power games.

This may happen whether we remain married to our first spouse, divorce and remain single, or begin a new relationship. It's just what children do as they grow up. In a new relationship we deal with it in the same way as we would if we had remained in our first marriage. Part of parenting is helping our children to become adults, and navigating the white water of emotional behaviour is part of the deal. We shouldn't confuse a flood of testosterone or oestrogen with them being unhappy with our new social life.

Are children selfish?

Is every issue that we have looked at in this chapter just about children's intrinsic selfishness? Can't they just be happy for us that we are making new friends? To answer both questions: children are as selfish as adults, and no, they can't just be happy for us because what we do affects them directly.

Parents provide a foundation for their children's lives as they grow up. When parents divorce, that foundation is cracked in two – and when a potential step-parent arrives, this person can never 'fill the gap'. Instead, they become part of a 'sideways extension' on one side of the crack. When both parents remarry, the children tend to establish themselves primarily upon one of the new foundations rather than equally on both.

Because the role of parents is 'foundational' children have little say in the process – and it is absolutely right that they shouldn't. Parents might ask their children for an opinion about a new friend, but they cannot ask their children to decide for them – that's putting an enormous and un-acceptable weight on young shoulders. What if they say 'I like this person' and it all ends in tears? They would then be to blame for future misery. No! Parents have to make their own choices in these matters and children understand this – they are, after all, used to being 'dependent'.

The issues which face children are not to be confused with selfishness. They probably want the best for us, but they are primarily, and rightly, concerned about their own future. If we change the foundations of their lives, it will affect them very directly.

Parenting

When it comes to introducing someone to our children (who they will think of as a potential new step-parent), we should be aware of what this is like from their point of view. If we understand how they feel, we can help them.

Some questions to think about

1. If I become a step-parent, what will the central issues be?
2. If my children become related to step-siblings, what will the central issues be?
3. How will we make sure that any children are secure, loved and parented?

12

Mentioning money

Is money the root of all marital evil? No, but it's a common source of friction, and once a divorce gets underway money matters can become very evil indeed. If our experience of divorce has been a financial nightmare, we may find it hard to be open with anyone about money. Don't lose heart though. Building a new relationship takes time, and if we use that time wisely we should be able to sort out financial decisions along the way.

If we are through the first three phases of bereavement (see Chapter 1) then our divorce is probably at least a year or two in the past. Straight after the divorce, we probably found that juggling our income and expenditure was akin to plate-spinning, but, after a while, we settled into a new 'economic pattern' – with earnings, benefits, maintenance and so forth all contributing to the total. As time went on, we probably even carved out a little pocket-money for ourselves. In effect, we became single again – not just maritally, but financially.

When a relationship develops

We have begun to make new friendships (and perhaps a new relationship) but we are still financially independent. If a relationship develops however, we shall, at some point, have to rethink our finances. The first bridge we have to cross is an emotional one: how do we feel about giving up our financial independence once again?

71

The second bridge we have to cross is entirely practical. If a relationship becomes permanent then joint incomes, financial provision and shared responsibilities may affect our disposable income. It's therefore worth taking a quick look towards the horizon and noting the kind of issues that may arise:

- a change of job
- a house move
- pension provision
- life insurance
- ownership of savings
- changes in child maintenance
- recalculation of benefits
- recalculation of university costs
- inheritance.

Sorting out our finances after a divorce is often very complex. When we build a new relationship, it may become even more complex because:

- one (or each) partner has continuing commitments to their previous marriage – which limits current resources;
- the new partnership provides a joint income which is used as the basis for recalculating levels of benefit (and so forth);
- existing family members (most usually children) may resent what they regard as 'their money' (and maybe 'their inheritance') being spent on others.

Forewarned is forearmed

Getting good advice about these issues is worth its weight in gold. If we have no idea what to expect, we may find ourselves under financial pressure – which can very quickly turn the stress levels in any relationship up to maximum. The principle is this: if we don't do the fact-finding early on, we make a rod for each other's backs.

Some questions to think about

1. Would a remarriage change my income, savings and pension?
2. Would the change be for the better – or for the worse?
3. What would it mean financially to remarry while my ex-spouse is still alive?

Conclusion

◄◦►

Cold feet or warm heart?

Each human being is an individual and every situation is different, but the issues which shape relationships are common to just about everyone. This book has explored the general experience of dating after divorce – but if it has seemed both familiar and personal, this proves the point. If it has helped to bring those experiences into focus, then so much the better, because when there is clarity it's easier to distinguish issues that can be dealt with privately from those that need the guidance and expertise of others.

There is one last question though, and it's this: if new friendships and relationships are accompanied by all this baggage, are they worth the risk? Perhaps it would be easier to give up any thoughts of another relationship and just accept the single life.

There are two answers to this final question:

1. Don't allow the difficult to smother the good

As we saw in the Introduction, when we divorce it's like rooting out a plant in the garden. Not only is there a gaping hole but shoots of the original plant come up all over the place. This is true whether we make a new relationship or remain single. Unless we attend to the old shoots when they appear they gradually take over everything else – even when we are on our own.

New friendships or relationships are like hothouses. Because they engage our emotions, they stimulate new growth and we 'blossom' – but they also stimulate the shoots from our previous relationship too. Therefore, whether we remain single or begin a new relationship the issues are the same – it's just that in the hothouse of a new relationship, they grow up more quickly.

So, in this respect, we can think of relationships as not only 'worth it' but also extremely good for us. We are forced to deal with issues which we would have to deal with sooner or later anyway, and we have someone to share the task with.

2. The course of true love ...

Relationships are at the very heart of our lives and not one of them is straightforward. Whether we think about relationships between parents and children, brothers and sisters, or husbands and wives there is a similarity – every one of them is hard work but worth it.

If relationships were straightforward there would be no such thing as counselling and half of the medical profession would be out of a job! When it comes to making new friends and new relationships we will always be learning something new. We may fall out and stop seeing each other, but while we are together we inevitably benefit from each other's company – even if all we learn is hard truth about ourselves, and, in the process, the lessons of life. If we think that any relationship will run completely smoothly, then we must be Martian – we are certainly not human.

Do new friendships and relationships highlight difficult issues? Of course they do. Are they worth it? Definitely, because both we and the other person are unique and precious.

Life is a journey worth making in the company of others.

A final reminder

Not every friendship becomes a romantic relationship – but every friendship is a special relationship in its own right. Making a new friend who remains 'just a friend' enriches our life and theirs.

If a friendship develops into love and marriage, it's tempting to think of this 'serious relationship' as 'replacing' the initial friendship. If we continue to pay attention to our underlying friendship though, the relationship will be the richer for it.

I hope that this book will be of use to everyone dating after divorce and risking romance, but whatever the future holds, just remember this – first and last; friends first!

Resources

Books

As a general rule, books about bereavement and the journey through the various phases of bereavement are helpful to divorcées, so a trip to the local bookshop may be very worthwhile.

The following are also invaluable guides to issues surrounding divorce and remarriage:

Marriage: Restoring our Vision, published by the Bible Reading Fellowship (BRF) (£7.99) and available through the **friends**first website. In this book, David Robertson examines biblical principles, challenges current practice, and unpacks difficult issues such as cohabitation, divorce and remarriage.

Healing the Hurt, Restoring the Hope, Suzy Yehl Marta, published by Rainbows (£12.99): This book, using the Rainbows approach (details on page 79), helps guide children and young people through times of divorce, death and crisis.

Top Tips for Making New Friends and Enjoying Successful Relationships, Katharine Gray, published by **friends**first Publishing (£15). With a wealth of practical and helpful advice, this is a unique guide to making the most of meeting new friends through organisations like **friends**first.

And on the lighter side:

The Romantic Movement, Alain de Botton, published by Picador (£7.99). In this delightfully funny, thought provoking novel, the characters unwittingly play power games as the psychology of men and women in love is explored.

Organisations

friendsfirst

Established in 1999 to help all sorts of single Christians develop friendships and relationships with other single Christians, this is a service for those who have never been married, as well as those who are separated, divorced and widowed. Whatever your marital status, **friends**first understands that companionship is one of the greatest human desires. The organisation is founded on the philosophy that all relationships are best established first and foremost in friendship. It is a very personalised service, offering support at every point of membership, enabling people who are looking for new friendships and relationships, to find and establish them in the most effective ways. Membership is open to people living in the UK and Ireland.

Telephone: 0121 427 1286
www.friends1st.co.uk

Aquila Care Trust

Helps men and women rebuild their lives as they work through their emotions following separation and divorce – the five phases mentioned on page 16 of this book.

Telephone Central Office: 01892 665524
www.aquilatrust.org

Diocese of Chelmsford

Offers help for the journey of separation and divorce, through a personal workbook, material for group discussion and a liturgy for divorce.

Contact Canon Sylvia Chapman: 01245 354479
e-mail: canons.chapman@btinternet.com

Rainbows

Rainbows is a non profit-making international organisation that provides training for establishing peer-support groups for children, adolescents and adults who have experienced a death, divorce or other painful transition in their family.

Telephone Central office: 01582 724106
www.rainbowsgb.org

Citizens Advice Bureau

Help with questions about benefits (and so forth), without charge.